A pinch of yarn

Kayur Patel

BookLeaf Publishing

India | USA | UK

Presentation by *BookLeaf Publishing*

Web: www.bookleafpub.com

E-mail: info@bookleafpub.com

ISBN: 978-93-5761-144-2

First edition 2022

DEDICATION

To all of the wanderers, and wonderers who feel lost. Lose yourself in yourself and you will find love.

ACKNOWLEDGEMENT

I thank the warriors and worriers who fight on each day to face the day with bruised hands, bloodied knuckles, broken smiles, bright eyes and beating hearts. The journey isn't guaranteed to be pleasant, but keep walking because the travelers just might surprise you.

PREFACE

What happens when all that is, meets itself?

Yarn Journeys

I remember a time when
I anchored my rope tightly to drifting clouds
I ventured off into the depths
I dove into unknowns just to see where they led
I returned with brand new eyes

I dove into each journey with no expectation of
there being another

That was then

Now those are but distant memories
expectations have also left my side and only
disappointment remains
Drifting clouds pass by day after day hoping to
be lassoed one more time

Now my mind is a place for silence.
Even the voices have stopped talking.
Bridges and cliffs no longer excite them, nor do
pills and knives
now they just sit in silence within the darkness,
consumed by it.

They have started to cheer for me

They, victim to their own game
They ask to be released from their suffering.

That yarn is collecting dust in the shadows
maybe it is time to tie the noose one more time
find a drifting cloud to hang from.

The Magician

Let there be light, from the sleeping night arises
darkness
From night, an aureate flicker shimmers through
the depths of space
waking dormant giants as if illuminating the
shrouded darkness

Let there be warmth, from the frozen abyss fire
dances out.
igniting the furnaces that lay dormant,
with hammer in hand the giants resume their
work

Let there be shape, with each strike of the anvil
the craftsmen begin crafting
First strike for the root, second for the crown,
third for the hold and last for the gold.

Let there be life, from the craftsmen sweat water
springs forth like a rainstorm
As each drop calms the tempered mold,
the dance of life takes center stage

Let there be freedom, the air around begins to
swirl

with each step and each twirl, spiral and spin it
picks up speed
building momentum, giving wings to those
shackled dreams.

"Try less, Be more"

Patience

A pindrop, a lightning strike, waterfalls and
charcoal
A heaviness that exists there only in the
moment.
Silence lifted like the slow rise of a curtain
Darkness retreats into the shadows as the light
from the gaze of on audience envelops the stage.

There in that moment you sit at the edge of
control.

Nerves on high, sweat coagulates into a pool
stuck to your body as if gravity is just a joke you
don't fully understand.

Your body shakes and trembles with the weight
of a fear you've tried to part ways with but like a
shadow it ceaselessly follows.

There in that moment a small breath escapes into
the last gasps of the silence that continues to lift.
You open your eyes, and add to the light

You begin filling in the outlined smile traced out
ten seconds into the future and you feel it again,
The surrender of all which holds you down,

You feel it again, the lightness of being

Seeds

In the cold dark eternal sky,
Father time sits in emptiness,
in stillness, with patience,
awaiting the gardener to water the seed once
again,
to go forth and brave the darkness.

To plant a seed and to water it is a labor of love.
In a world of immediate gratification,
to expect the fruit before it is planted.
To have everything at fingertips before the click
of a button
The day when that possibility becomes real
draws near.

Chinese bamboo takes almost 5 years to grow.
imagine planting and watering it regularly for 5
years without any reward or confirmation of
labor?

Then at the moment of earthbreak, it shoots up
into the sky.
It grows almost two feet in a single day.
From nothing to an explosion of love.

Five years of navigating the darkness
underneath,
spreading far and wide building a rooted net
Then like a rocket aimed at the furthest star it
springs forth.

I fear the day when immediate gratification
simply becomes gratification because
"immediate" is too much of a delay.
On that day Patience will retreat into the depths
of time and space
and take the seed of love along with it.

The plunge into the darkness must be taken.
If you do not take the risk, the result will be far
more catastrophic than any kind of wild anarchy
that can be conceived,
so go forth and brave the darkness.
Seek the eternal teacher,
the world seed awaits.

Cursed beauty

Beauty is a curse
Beholders ignorant of their judgments
Baseless opinions showcasing the surface
Blind to the cruelty sleeping within
Battles raging
Between acceptance and self-worth, a
Balancing act on the tight rope of societal
pressure.
Braving each step, a caution of three kids
sneaking past three-headed dogs
Bluffing courage with a smile, while fear
Ballets across the forehead raising lines of
worry.
Barres are no place for men to explore their
grace,
Bars are where they
Belong placing
Bets on the next race.

The lovers

I chase the fading colors of sunday sunsets
I stand under the light of silence.

A whisper of leaves, the dance of trees.
A sea of glimmer, a veiled shimmer, as droplets
spark, a lover speaks.

"When and where did we go cold? I thought I
had you on hold."
A soft breeze approaches, release and let the
blood flow, just breathe, be free and fold.
Open hands a miracle lands.

Lightbringer

Rays of hope we call them
Those small beams of light breaking through the
atmosphere on their descent to the earthly
planes.
Those warriors who stand watch over the bitter
dark.

Shadow army grows stronger with each passing
day,
sheltered by night tendrils replacing retreating
rays.
As the last line of defenders brace for
encroaching darkness,
Faithkeepers pray to distant stars for
illuminating guidance.
Keep your faith and the light will never fade.

As day falls and night breaks through
the scales tip once again.
There in the imbalance, lifted by the shifting
lightness
she stands.
The lightbringer

To close a window

To close a window requires an immense amount
of strength.
If you're used to being outside, the indoor space
may scare you.
In knowing of life happening outside, being in
your prison may bring you comfort.
If listening to the sounds of nature calms you,
being in your machined existence may bring you
dread.
Close the window and experience yourself.
Close the window and sit with the darkness, not
merely in it.
With the darkness you'll find that you're not
alone.
The voices are louder as their echoes reverberate
throughout the enclosure.
The dreams are brighter as their light shutters
through each image more vividly
The smells are more pungent as the aroma has
no crevice to escape through.
Most important of all, you are not alone.

All of which escapes into the dark during
daylight seeks refuge in the shadows.

Seek their sanctuary
Refugee of battles waged throughout the day
Build your nest in the depths of uncharted
waters.
They have carved out a place only you can click
into, so be strong
Close the window.

The warrior

When you're in the middle of the battle
when all you can see is yourself, all of the
demons
standing against you on the battlefield
there will
inevitably
be an overwhelming feeling of dread and gloom.
Hopelessness creeps up
because no matter how many of them you fight
off
they keep coming in an endless supply

but what you are often blind to is the fact that
you're not fighting alone
even if you are feeling alone in the middle of
that arena, the effort isn't futile
you're still withering the enemy forces one at a
time.

Something can be said about elephants and bites,
the same about Davids and Goliaths

I know that the world and life feels particularly
impossible to change right now

but there are forces working with us beyond our
control and comprehension.
All that is left is faith, and faith will always
remain.

Faith that the tide will continue to turn as it
always has.
The world has yet to encounter a day when
waves refuse to return to the ocean after kissing
the shoreline.
The sand can not keep water at bay
nor does the ocean have authority to prevent
waves from embracing the shore.
Whether you're traveling to the shore or back to
the ocean.
Just have faith and ride the wave.

To hold a door

Holding a door open is a selfless act.
That small moment, noticing another being
crossing through the same threshold.
Entering a place, you meet someone new every
time
The vessel may look familiar, the being inside
will be new
They will have gone on a journey through time
since your last interaction
They will have walked through the dark
They will have awaken to a new sun
They will have closed their eyes surrounded by
demons, with nothing more than faith.
So will you.

To hold a door open is a selfless act,
in that moment, you acknowledge a fellow
traveler, you notice their journey, and you
choose to make their journey one step lighter.

Law and Order

Beyond the illusion of senses,
Beyond the traffic of thoughts
Beyond the reward of action. I am you are I

A beating drum holds silence as much as an
earthquake holds stillness.
The sky holds clouds as much as the ocean holds
water.
"kindly let me help you or you'll drown" said the
monkey safely putting the fish on the tree.

I cheer for the underdog because I see myself in
that ring,
I shy away from your eyes because I see my
pain in your tears
I walk through the forest at night because I know
what lies within my darkness

Input: I am a poet
Practice: I write poems
Output: Poetry

Vision boards take us far into the future,
reality keeps us rooted in the present
patience connects the two dots

A seed is one tree's way of becoming another
Birth is life's way of experiencing death
You are my way of being you

If crashing waves scare you, do not throw rocks
into still waters
If you release snakes into a neighbors farm,
sleep with an antidote under your pillow
If respecting women is important, avoid
regulating their bodies

A farmer who plants for himself will live a
lonely life
A farmer who plants for his family will live a
healthy life
A farmer who plants for his community will live
a happy life

I am I because you are you
The sky is up because the earth below
Yesterday and tomorrow are one step from today

Why does the calm always end?
Why is it chased by a storm?
Why love if pain is sure to follow?

On a rotating rock revolving around a spinning
star,

expecting things to remain constant is an
impossible dream
May the dream remain impossible because
without change only death remains

Sun rays energize
Moon beams soothe
Give and receive

Archways

Am I just pretending? Should I return to a
simple life.
Waking up everyday, a cup of tea sloshing
around in the cupholder on my commute to
work.
Spend my morning teaching tiny humans how to
make learning fun,
train their imagination to see beyond what their
eyes are capable of.
Spend my evenings with larger tiny humans
teaching them how to make life a little more
bearable,
opening space for their hidden tiny humans to
roam free in larger bodies.
All the while pretending to practice those skills
for myself.

Most days are spent in the emptiness,
not the kind that once brought clarity,
this new kind brings unwanted attention.
I can hear the fridge buzzing, but the bees no
longer speak to me.
I can feel the fan whirling it's blades, but the
wind no longer dances on my body

I can taste the bitterness of my saliva, but the
water no longer is sweet
I can see the darkness in broad daylight, but the
moon no longer looks bright
I can touch the roughness of my skin, but i can
no longer feel.
Am I just pretending to be human because my
mechanical heart pulses to 1s and 0s.
On off, on off, tick tock. That is all a pulse is. a
reminder that one second you are on, and the
next you are off.
Rinse and repeat until one day the switch is left
permanently on or off.
What is the difference?
Do we ever know in our last moment, if we left
the light on or off?

A simple life. What a joke.
Nothing about it is simple, and it was never
meant to be.
The moment I crossed that threshold,
the moment I walked under that archway, simple
remained behind.

Death in your eyes

You have beautiful eyes and it scares me
I keep these words locked inside because I want
to be scared
Your beauty lies deep within, deep beauty scares
me

It rests in the void, the journey inwards excites
me
It is novel, high inducing
I don't take it for the high, I take it to be seen, to
see

I venture inwards to find you, the real you
Not the one graced by the silver reflection
outside
The real you, bathing in the light of black abyss
inside.

You have beautiful eyes and looking into them
scares me
If I look too long, I will lose myself on the quest
of finding you

Waves

Lighting strikes for one last time on the horizon,
roaring blues meet silenced blacks
The chaos storm subsides into exhaustion
Rain clouds slowly dissipate into the void,
arrows of light pierce through the lifting veil.

Her vibrant face strikes through to the heart of
the abyss
A cold quiet calm settles into waves of calamity
As stillness binds water into silence,
Floating driftwood whispers stories of madness
Ships holding hopes of futures and promises
ripped apart,
fractured rafts float aimlessly

The dawning sun kisses each piece of wreckage
Atop a lonely floating splinter, a dove bathes in
warm rays
It scans the wreckage one last time, opens its
wings and takes flight
Flap those wings and be free.

Love locked

Several ages ago, I foolishly thought all poems
were love poems.
Convinced by that notion, all of my poems were
love poems.
I would write love, poems
I would write about my love for poems
I would write about love in my poems
Love and poems, it just seem to fit like lock and
key

Now I seem to have misplaced the key and love
is bound in chains by a lock.

The tower

Men are playing my games
Women are playing mind games
Both are playing I games
We've been tricked into playing eye games

If my mind could see what my eye is blind to,
I am simply playing my game

Hope

Hope is a powerful illusion
It turns the wisest of sages into naïve fools
Any wise person knows that hope is just fear in
disguise
The wolf in sheep's clothing may fool the sheep
but the shepherd always knows
Yet when the time comes, even the shepherd is
tricked, and the wolf gets away.

This is the way it has to be, or else sheep would
never follow shepherds

Why I write

"What it is to be between a rock and a hard
place" as the words hit the page,
I was struck from behind.
I sat in traffic appreciating the moons beauty
ahead
the golden sun showing off in the rear view
mirror.

I stepped out to asses the damage and noticed a
kid still sitting in his car looking down at his
phone,
No attempt to acknowledge my presence or
apologize for his mistake.

I moved my car out of the way to avoid a jam in
morning traffic,
He took that opportunity to begin his escape.
I drove in front to block his path and he finally
stepped out.

"If you have something to say then say it, but
there ain't shit on your car"
"Can I see your license please?"
"I got my license right here but there ain't shit on
your car"

We both stepped back into our vehicles, I
snapped a picture with my phone and carried on
with our days.
I sat gleefully with that experience in my head
for the rest of the day.
In that moment I knew that he will sit with the
fear of being reported for much longer than I
will sit with his disrespect.

There is no damage to my car because damn that
beauty knows how to take a beating. I
contemplated reporting him to keep his ego in
check, but I know I will not to keep mine in
check.

This is why I write. Sometimes the poem is
written before your pen reaches the paper.
Sometimes you are the pen the universe is
writing through.
Sometimes in your travels, you've dropped
breadcrumbs a long the way to help you find
your way back home.

You may not see them
you may not smell them
you may not hear them
or even feel them

They lay dormant, waiting to be grazed by the
tip of your finger
as they awaken and reorient back together,
they wait for the next yarn journey to get lost in,
they wait for the next forest to mark your
footfalls.